if this is Armageddon
– it's very pretty

First published in 2000
Reprinted in 2001

bradshaw books
Tigh Filí (Poets' House)
Thompson House
MacCurtain Street
Cork, Ireland
Phone +353 21 4509274
Fax +353 21 4551617
e-mail admin@cwpc.ie

British Library Cataloguing in Publication Data
ISBN 0 949010 63 4

Cover design by Nick Sanquest/Fiona Heraghty
Typeset and layout at Tigh Filí
Printed and bound by Lee Press, Cork

if this is Armageddon
– it's very pretty

Liz Willows

bradshaw books
Cork

To P and J,
W K and
"... blessed be the women who get (me) through"

Robin Morgan

Acknowledgements

My thanks to all who made this first collection possible, all at
Tigh Filí who have supported me, particularly Máire
Bradshaw for her courage and vision; Catherine Creedon and
Ian Wild for constructive editing; Nick Sanquest for manning
the lifeboat; Feargha Ní Bhroin, Claire Horgan, Steve Toms
and Tim O'Sullivan for blatant groupyism when it mattered.
A special acknowledgement to hayley FOX roberts for an
inspiring and exciting poetry partnership.

Contents

Toward the Millinerium

I've been making hats this week
endlessly snipping, pinning, and
sewing little hats.
With a vague idea of
making money on the side
– even starting a new trend
if I get good enough.
It's funny but I'd never
imagined myself a milliner.

My daughter said today
they look like lampshades
and it occurred to me that
she's right, they do.
I'd been quite pleased until then,
you know, a new line in creativity,
something I could do without having
first been taught.
Natural talent!

But... it's true
I'm never going to gain renown
by making hats
that look like lampshades.

A Sense of Place

Higher than my head stray stalks
of unharvested flax seem
to mock me with the spirits
of Kavanagh
and the poets of Ulster
for my Englishness
and therefore lack of soul.

I could walk forever
the briar edged road,
with budding daffodil and marsh marigold
waiting for the magic to
slide over my left shoulder.
The poet's birthplace shrieks
PRIVATE – NO ADMITTANCE
in blue & white hostility
as I try to imagine
the window from which
young Patrick pondered
his father's backside.

The Muse is nipping
at my red city
ankles as I curse the formality
of my English tongue
while the Monaghan ranges
hide themselves always
around the next bend of the road.

If there were a mountain
in sight I could believe
I were in Keswick then
the poetry of my
schooling would give me
a host of flaming
daffodils instead of the flaxen
ghosts who look into my veins
and see no race memory
of their history.

A Game for Two Players

Please let's not play Mastermind
(or Mstressmind)
in bed at 3 a.m. It could be warm
and snuggly here wrapped in each other.

Rapt in each other after love-making
I'm too exhausted for questioning
the ethics of why we're here.
I know why I'm here:

it's my bed and it's bed-time.
Sorry – I got the answer wrong again.
Why are you here?
Oh – I hadn't realised I'm not allowed

to question the questioner.
Why does sex create so many questions
when I thought it held all the answers?
Pass.

Would Ogden Nash approve?

Would Ogden Nash approve
my telling of how the
seeds of cultivated flowers,
purple anemone, white aubretia,
have escaped over the garden walls?
Planting themselves in the cracks
of the pavement –
they can't be tamed.

My heart is this way,
escaping the narrow confines
of what is supposed to be,
loving where it will;
'Very Like a Whale'.

Geri

You are so beautiful to me
as you lie there
learning to die the way
you learned to live as a baby.

Come to me now,
let me hold your hands
and tell you.
You are so beautiful to me.

I once found a photograph
of Amelia Earhart and she could
have been your twin.
Learn to fly now.

Knowing you have done all you could
for this place.
The place for you now
is away from here. Leap.

We hold hands as I see
the mother wolf labouring
under the full moon to bring
her cub to life.

You emerge panting.
You are so beautiful to me.
I will only let go after you leave,
how easy to break that promise.

Your will ever stronger than mine.
Your creativity flowing through me,
my children yours and I your child,
mother hold me now.

Like an infant I mewl, lost,
the most beautiful to me,
gone. I emerge motherless
in the cold full moon.

Fragmentation

I sit and
try to write
a poem.
I am a mother.
I am a sister, a daughter, a carer, a lover.

GET – READY – FOR – BED

The massed amounts
of a day
spent listening to the old.
Listening to The Old Grey Whistle Test.
Trying to like my brother's favourite music.
Trying to like my brother.

THERE'S A CLEAN NIGHTIE IN YOUR NIGHTIE
DRAWER –
PIPPA – STOP THUNDERING...

on the stairs.
The thunder threatened to come
today and
– all we had in common
was our musical taste
especially as his conservative stance
was pure.
Purely done to wind me up.

ARE – YOU – TRYING – TO – DRIVE – ME – CRAZY?
BOILED – EGG – AND – TOAST – FINGERS

it used to be battery egg and soldiers
until awareness got the better of me
– and I'll have to wake the baby up
the heat has made him sleep
but perhaps I'll write
the poem later, in a
quiet moment,
as a letter to my brother?
And I never did the washing –
the thunder threatened rain.

Will the poet try again,
awakening in fifteen years or so?
But the muse may
have died by then.

All day I thought
there was a poem.
There was a poem I wanted.
There was a poem I wanted to write.

One Relationship...

1

The 23rd of April
is the anniversary
of Shakespeare's birth,
St George's day,
Kath Fraser's birthday
and the day you came to do your washing
at my house –
I know which is
most important.

2

We kissed
KAPOW!
The earth moved.

It is still trembling
a year later.

3

It's not the same
without you to
make a brew.
I drink a lot less now.

Fire

Our lovemaking blinds
me with orange light. Sacral
chakra. It overwhelms
and envelops me.

My fiery lover's touch burns
hot on my breast, belly, cunt 'til
I am tempted to look for scorched
flesh, witch's burn, branded.

I drown in molten rivers, heedless.
Clammy skin sucking, breast
flattened against chest.

Our love-making cracks
the ice of our midwinter sheets.
Melting the frost on
the windows for the duration.

Willow

Oh! How the mighty are fallen –
after thinking I was god or
the devil for an eternity
I found myself in the same
sordid world as the rest of you –
where homophobes shriek abuse
outside Centra (and even work inside).
Feeling afraid I don't answer back but
walking faster, cheeks flushing with shame
that surely isn't mine.

Oh! How the mighty are fallen –
after thinking I was the devil or
god for an eternity
I find myself in the same
serene world as the rest of you –
taking my own space
growing upwards and outwards
like a willow, though surely no sylph.

Oh! How the fallen become mighty –
supple and bending, spreading
over and onwards each delicate
green leaf a new feeling
each fragile green feeling a new leaf
in the rewrite of the rest of my life
no bible in my garden of hades to
guide or accuse but those other
travelling journeywomen whose names
are shouted unheard.

Holding the Fort

"...Three years after the end of the First World War the trenches were inhabited by rats, lizards, weasels and the as yet unburied remains of the dead..." Documentary – BBC Radio 4

I have spent many years inhabiting graves
crawling round the decomposed remains
dwelling in an 'other world'
ignored by the living
as the dead were abandoned.

Call me vampire but I never
sucked the blood of any living thing
and I like to think that my presence
was small comfort to the souls of those
caught up in never-ending screech of mortar.

Those who survived the trench experience
came home shattered, crippled with
rotting feet and scrambled wits
shaking in the permanent pounding
shells shocking, never-ceasing fire.

Call these the lucky ones then,
whose bones remain without rites,
with a white cross to mark
a resting place never reached.
Small comfort the scavenging creatures.
The small and hot-blooded
or the quickening reptile
keeping watch, bearing witness, holding the fort.

Splash

Hook, line and sinker I fell,
was caught, enmeshed.
Fish hook snared on the soft palate.

The barbed lure,
bitter... sweet? Pain.
All a bit S/M for what I had in mind.

What can you expect though?
When all we ever did was
talk barbed words,
hooking into flesh –
teeth bite.

I was hooked, a hooker
captured me, selling herself
at my cost. I her pimp
to use and amuse,

floundering, painfully out of my depth,
got thrown back into the water –
Plenty more fish in the sea, love.

World AIDS Day 1999

I'd like to name all of those
I've loved and lost –
but they're not all mine for the naming
(Those ones that I've loved who stayed
were never mine for the taming).
The litany of names grows
louder each year,
more candles to light. The
furnace of my grieving pyre glows
ever brighter threatening
to implode leaving
me, a black hole.
Tenacious is my name and I
will not let go of my dead yet.

I Didn't Scream at Birth

My aversion to water
I'm sure
comes from having been drowned
at birth –
in the womb.
Being thrust out of security
the greedy baby
sucked too soon
filling my lungs with the waters
of the womb
      life came hard that day
as a still-born baby
blue as if drowned in a river
emerged
      still-life means death
and for all of three minutes or more
remained dead
waiting for the midwife's pronouncement of
      still-life means death
      still-birth no life
and still
      life/spirit lingered
water poured forth
gushing a small cupful
of infant mortality
SPARKLED in the sunlight
SPLATTERED against the living room wall
and with it
fate sealed the bargain
"This life is yours".

Letter to the Collective

Sorry the cheque bounced.
The bank manager needed proof
that we can pay it back soon
and as you have pointed out,
I have no income.

The £38,500 house that you insisted
I get a mortgage on
while you paid the deposit
(just to make sure that working-class women would
own property too,
so that your public Marxism needn't suffer)
isn't selling
and when it does I'll have
maybe as much as £2,500
to squander
on my
debts of £3,000
– which includes your £500
so that's a problem.
But hang about –
here's the thing,
if I don't pay you back
it'll all balance out.

Wanting You

I want you!
Here in this café
sitting across from you,
leaning in, to hear
the quietness of you.
I want you –

not in any metaphysical way;
no subtlety here in my longing.
I want you –
now!

As your nipples tease me through the
thin fabric of your
blue and white striped
shirt...Oh! I want you here
in the space where my head
loses all thought and instead
my fingers and tongue do
the sensing, tasting, touching of you.

I ask if you'd like to lick ice-cream
from the insides of my thighs –
knowing what your response will be:
Stop! you say,
pleading against the upsurge of sensation
Would you though?
I persist with all the cockiness
of knowing my conquest.

Stop! you're begging –
which you know by now only
incites me to greater boldness.

I describe my desire more fully
leaning across, hushed tones,
some semblance of privacy
where our whole body language speaks of
I want you!

Rocking on my chair I can hardly
contain this exploding urge
to take you here
pushing you down onto
the polished, well-trodden floorboards
where half-a-dozen people are
spending a quiet Friday afternoon.
I want you.

All the while in my imagination
I bite and lick and pull at
your teasing nipples through the light fabric.
Undoing your buttons and sliding
my hand inside as
I raise my mouth to yours
bearing my weight down as
you lie passively beneath me
– so now we know it's a fantasy –
but still I want you.

I want my hands sliding across your ass
opening you up to me...
Now it's me pleading –
Come home with me?
You accept your power gracefully –
Yes, I want you too.

Sadomasochism

1

The light in her eye
belies the set of her face
as she stands above me
teasing, testing.
I bound
wrists above
ankles spread
watch thrilled
as she teases
tests,
playing out the fantasy
we created
together.
Trust, warmth, love
flow from my cunt
as she touches
tests, teases.
Love, warmth, trust
flow back,
interact,
    intertwine
between and through us.

2

Another time.
  Another place.
    Another lover.
Sweating, gulping
tongue aching
she pushes
      her cunt in my face,
      my face in her cunt
for
thirty minutes?
An hour?
A lifetime?
          Here,
until
she angry
pushes me away –
It's no good, I can't come!
I'm still upset
you didn't agree with me
at the meeting.
What's your definition
of Sadomasochism?

21

The Housewife's Guide to The Rolling Stones

The only time I
stop moving is
when my brain
is tangled with

what's the next job?
Wash the nappies, or the dishes?
Change the beds? Feed the fishes?
Will I vacuum? Do the shopping?
Start the dusting? Now I'm hopping
from one foot to the other –
Do I pick the kids up,
or ring my lover?
Feed the cats? Shake the mats?
Walk the dog? Scour the bog?
Mend that shelf, or
be myself?

Roll a cig, brew up, read a book,
write a poem, have a long lazy
bath, even think about making love.
But none of those have any of the rhythm of the above.

Successful home management
rests mainly with those
who gather no moss.

Writing the Handbook

I always meant to write you a poem.
This morning I read:
If today was the last day of your life
what would you have wanted to do with it?
I want to write a poem for you.
My son, my baby, youngest of three
and born at the wrong time I thought,
having buried your brother
the year before.
But timing is never wrong Jordan,
my Jo. Jo-Jo that you're too
old for, and makes you cringe.
You came along at just the right moment.

The right moment to share in my grief and loss,
the right moment to share in my addiction,
the right moment to share in my healing,
the right moment to help me learn to feel.
Jordan, my Jo. Jo-Jo.
Life so incomprehensible to your outlook
that people just be nice, and fair.
I wish, my love, for you that they were.
People are people, and as you grow
seeing all the misery of other's sickness
 – carrying it for them –
bullies, addicts and the soul-destroyed,
you keep on smiling. My beautiful son.

Generous, even when hungry for so much.
Surviving in a world at odds with your envisioning,
you know you are loved.
Even though I don't have all the skills to show it, yet.

Martin

My ex-lover, who is a man, carried
our baby's coffin to his grave – stumbling.
Later... pissed from one glass of whisky
I collapsed on the bathroom floor,
almost dead I tried to die.

My ex-lover, who is a gay man, kicked
the door down, macho style, and
carried me to my bed.
My body lay there. I tried to die.

Watching as if from two miles distance
were my eyes.
Watching the still, cold form on the bed try for death
– my long distant friend.

My long-distant friend the Methodist
minister's daughter said a name – but
I couldn't hear. Shouted a name –
I wouldn't hear.
Slapped the face on the body   L I Z
SNAPPED BACK HURT HURT
RED HOT RAGE HURT STRANGLED
STRANGLING ON SALT BLOOD BILE I
HURT I HURT I
OH MY GOD MY BABY'S DEAD AND THE PARTY'S
IN FULL SWING.

Drink more whisky, roll another joint,
we even gave my mother one.
An hysterical party in honour of Martin –
named for a bird, he flew away after
fourteen months. I should have guessed.

I looked at my daughter – still living;
at my ex-lover – still living;
at myself – still living;
futures, still to be lived.
My mother ate toast all day
and a sister brought a hundred cigs
thinking we may be in need. Oh yes.
Everyone sat, talked, laughed, moved forward.

To know me now
you have to know that
Martin's death made me.
The woman you see now –
the dyke in a dress with raw bulging eyes
and tinted glasses for concealment,
the grief-ridden lonely woman
who feels sorry for herself
so writes poetry for comfort,
– she didn't exist before Martin died.

Cathy

Friday night we both arrived down in Cork.
From Dublin and Kerry, separately. Unannounced.
Catching up on long-time-no-see friends.

Do you remember that awful woman?
The one who wanted me to take her home, but
scared the living daylights out of me.
You saved me then
and came with me instead.

I remember now how you danced that night,
knowing I could picture you in your underwear.
Coming home under the full Scorpion moon
you howled idiotically all the way and,
because I loved you I wasn't embarrassed.
You pointed out your favourite star and told me
how your funeral should be ordered.

Monday morning parting. Until the next time.
Making plans for your trip to Kerry,
your Dublin jokes about needing wellies.
I got the card with the baby on it –
fancying me pregnant by your lust.

I wrote back sending you the first instalment
of a story you asked me to write.
We thought we'd meet in Galway, but
you stayed home to work. And then you were killed.
How did that happen?

Sandra

I still imagine Sandra
in the deep blue velvet dress
with white Peter Pan collar.

Sandra's mum
finding it all too much
put Sandra's head in the gas oven
along with those
of her two brothers –
a strange meat and two veg –

after giving them a sleepytime drink
of hot chocolate and tranquillisers –
they were all under six
so would have fit quite nicely.

After tucking her children up
making sure they'd never wake
Sandra's mum threw herself out
of the upstairs bedroom window
breaking both her legs.

Duncan

Dancing to Stiff Little Fingers
with Duncan,
leaping wildly, cavorting,
colliding. The last photograph
taken of him is at a party
in my home
the week before his death.

Sitting in a chair, wrapped and bound in wool,
a child's potty on his head, and a copy
of *Playgirl* open on his lap. Dead drunk,
dead to the world. Can of lager in hand.
That was the night I noticed blood in his ears.

How can you offer a mother a picture like that?
We didn't. Collecting money
from his mates in the Carlton pub
in Standish Street, we found a florist
who made a wreath. A replica of the illustration
from the centre of his favourite album,
Join Hands by Siouxsie and the Banshees.

His coffin was kept closed after all,
as his peacock tribe
of punk friends
gathered with his open-hearted family
at the crematorium
in Burnley, Lancashire.
Where for once only
the scratched copy of
the 23rd psalm
was outweighed by
SLF and *Suspect Device*.

Platonism

This poem wasn't meant to be written
at 3:24 a.m. (according to my red-eyed
electric alarm clock). I don't think it was
meant to be written at all.

I couldn't find the pen
beneath all the books
which habitually surround my bed.
My cigarette diminished and died,
abandoned breathless in the ashtray.
The corner of the duvet drank tea
in the feckless candlelight...

and the woman by my side
so easily asleep –
provoking my insomnia
– shifted, and spoke.
I found my pen,
cautioned sleep to my friend,
and started to write,
rather than seduce.
Averting a disaster.

Out on a Limb

There's me, hanging off the tree.
Out on a limb again.
I can't be a coward – however hard I try.

Loving where I will,
less skill than importunity,
leaping off the cliff – as if both of us might fly.

The sweetest "*no*" I ever heard,
I swear that I too am afraid,
unable to be a liar – fired with a passion.

For all my eccentricities,
I'm really quite old fashioned.
But fit a scold upon my tongue – ration

my foolishness. Wrong this
time, this place. I have to face
that this is God's will – not mine.

One Love Poem

Silenced – eventually –
by you saying *I love you*
I longed to respond with equal depth
 – or even fatuous cliché –
but I looked at you,
and fell silent.

Back home I slurped over-ripe plums
writing poetry.
The juice went up my nose and
dribbled down my chin as
I struggled for a metaphor
to describe

to capture you in words;
the way Rich's 'VIII'
captivated us both.

Breathless, voiceless in the presence
of the wordsmith who wove
the warp. I am clumsy in my efforts
to express a promise. A working
of an old story in a new tongue –
and I fall silent.

Proper Order

I nearly rang you, wanting
to share the sunset,
remembering in time that you
are not that way inclined.

Could I have rung you instead
sharing the cool honesty
of I miss you.
I know that you would say yes.

If I can gaze on the sunset
here, knowing that you also
share this sky with thoughts
of me, intimacy remains.

Another Bloody Love Poem

Why did so many poets
write about love
before I had a chance
to meet you?

Now, all my feelings
are dressed in the words
of others. Instead – describing all the
newness and ingenuity you inspire
in me, I hear a thousand
cliché's tumble out clumsily.

Reflection

Pity the thirteen-year-old
as she arrives in school
bedraggled and unloved.
Look in her eyes.
The other children point fingers,
jeering as she's hauled before
the principal and named *Slut*.

Listen to the child talking
with authority about blow-jobs
to the boys on the run from remand.
Between the lines she wishes she were
Enid Blyton's "George";
Gobbler is her name.

Have compassion for the little girl
who takes alcohol and Valium in
exchange for sex with strangers –
just to feel someone's arms around her.
It's hard. They call her *Easy*.

Pity the thirteen-year-old
who passes off her semen stained
school skirt as soiled
with Horlicks from the café where
she works. *Whore-licks* the other
kids call her.

Let your pity bathe her, cleanse her.
Galvanise her.
Bring her into adulthood.
Name her. Call her. *Me*.

Colouring by Numbers

I like a good sky.
I'll point it out saying:
Look at that – what a sky!
As my loved ones join in the
appreciation – or humour me.

There have been some great skies
lately, real biblical numbers. You
know – broiling multi-coloured clouds
in impossible unnamed shades where
all you are waiting for is God's
voice booming and His finger pointing
(and I've seen both of those recently too).

My only trepidation is that
all this ariel flamboyance is a sign,
that all those bloody 'Millennium
Doom' merchants are right.
But, if this is Armageddon – it's very pretty.

Also available from bradshaw books:

ŏ

bradshaw books
Order Form

Name:
Address:

Tel:
Fax:
E-mail:

Title of book:
No. of copies:

Please return to
bradshaw books, Tigh Filí, MacCurtain St,
Cork.
Tel: 353 21 450 9274
Fax: 353 21 455 1617
E-mail: admin@cwpc.ie

See our complete list of publications on our
website at www.tighfili.com